About the Author

Dalton Kusaselihle Dladla is a gold-hearted person who likes to inspire people through motivation. He aims to give hope to others who have lost it. Dladla is passionate about encouraging people not to give up in life.

How to Keep the Candle Burning Through the Storm

Dalton Kusaselihle Dladla

How to Keep the Candle Burning Through the Storm

Olympia Publishers
London

www.olympiapublishers.com
OLYMPIA PAPERBACK EDITION

Copyright © Dalton Kusaselihle Dladla 2024

The right of Dalton Kusaselihle Dladla has been asserted in accordance with sections 77 and 78 of the Copyright, Designs and Patents Act 1988.

All Rights Reserved

No reproduction, copy or transmission of this publication
may be made without written permission.
No paragraph of this publication may be reproduced,
copied or transmitted save with the written permission of the publisher,
or in accordance with the provisions
of the Copyright Act 1956 (as amended).

Any person who commits any unauthorised act in relation to
this publication may be liable to criminal
prosecution and civil claims for damage.

A CIP catalogue record for this title is
available from the British Library.

ISBN: 978-1-83543-307-2

This is a work of fiction.
Names, characters, places and incidents originate from the writer's imagination. Any resemblance to actual persons, living or dead, is purely coincidental.

First Published in 2024

Olympia Publishers
Tallis House
2 Tallis Street
London
EC4Y 0AB

Printed in Great Britain

Dedication

I dedicate this book to my late father, David Dladla, and my lovely wife, Mrs. E.Z. Dladla, the pillar of my strength. Thank you for loving me, apple of my eye.

Acknowledgments

I would like to thank my wife, who has been supporting me. Thank you for being my integral part.

INTRODUCTION

In life, you are like the candle burning, and life is like a storm. No matter how strong the storm is, you need to keep the candle burning through it. Don't let the candle's flame die. This book is a beacon of hope. It will prepare you for every situation you come across and light a fire under you.

After reading this book, your life will be energized and rejuvenated. Remember, you cannot learn how to walk or run if you allow basophobia, because you fall down several times before mastering both. Most successful people have lost their footing, stumbled, and fell down several times. It is undeniable that human beings learn from their mistakes. Failing does not mean it's over, but its simple meaning is to go back to your drawing board, re-strategize, and put your new strategy into the test.

Remember, cars are assembled in well-lit areas, under the roof and flat areas, but they are equipped with headlights, gears, clutch, brake, hand brake, accelerator and so on, because the makers anticipate the situations the car will go through. Whenever your life is driving through darkness, switch on your head lights; whenever you want to go faster, accelerate and change to higher gear that suits your desired speed. When you are driving in a steep slope situation, use your brake and downshift to reach the desired velocity.

God knew what we would come across while we were fetuses and prepared us to withstand every situation we would come across. All we need to do is to keep the consuming fire burning within us and emerge victoriously. God said, "If you abide in me and my words abide in you, whatever you ask shall be provided."

1
All That I Am

I listen to good music to write the good one.
I read the Bible to write my own one.
I celebrate people's lives for my life to be celebrated.
I believe that being selfless and
Making positive impact to other people's lives is the key
To open flood gates of blessings for me.
I believe that I was born to lead.
I believe that confrontation is the cure and gossiping is
poison.
I live for what I believe is right,
I believe to keep on fighting until what I believe is mine
Is handed over to me.
I believe there is no such thing as a free lunch,
Even Jesus Christ was crucified for redemption
Of other people's sins.
I have met different challenges that test my strength and
Make me stronger.
I fall day by day; however, I never quit,
I never lay down, I never surrender,
I never lose faith and hope, and I will never give up,
No matter how hard things may become,
I am going to reach my destiny.
There is time in life where you may think
The sun will never shine on you.
However, the fact is that it will shine on you one day,

'Cause every dog has its day.
One day, there will be no stone of an offender
That will be left unturned,
Where the victims will be crowned.
Am I carrying the cross of dismissal?
Yes, it is not easy, but it is worth it.
Was I dismissed by a mistake?
No. If it was not me, who would be?
The offenders think I am going to run like a headless chicken.
Thank you for being with me in time of need, Almighty God.
You showed me my strength.
Thank you for the person I am, I will never wish to be
Somebody else.
I love myself and I am proud for being the person who I am,
Regardless of bad chapter of my life I'm going through right now.
No matter how people look down on me,
I am not going to lose my self-recognition.
No matter the misjudgment I received from people,
I do not mind and
I will keep my head up and I will be Dk for life.

2

In Human Life, There Are Mountains, Steep Slopes, Flat Areas And There Are Also Seasons

There is a time in life where you find your journey to be challenging,
Where in life you find rough and intimidating mountains to climb up,
Where you also find the weather not pretty good for you,
Where you need to face the reality and persevere toward the mountain's peak.

There is also a nice and flat journey,
Where things are pretty good for you,
Where you can feel that you are from royalty.
You also need to prepare yourself for the next season.
At times, you may find yourself walking in snow,
Where frostbite is challenging you,
Where you recognize the importance of sunny summer days,
Where you need to maintain the pace and keep going.
When you are in pain,
You must know that there is a pain-free time that is coming for you.
When your journey becomes more difficulty, you must know

that it will be over,
You need to keep pressing on and be what you want to be.

Sky is the limit for those who aim for the moon.
There is a price for every runner,
the bigger price lies on performance.
If you run like a hero,
You will be crowned and honored like a king.
Outstanding performance deserves excellent pay.

3

The Aeroplane

Fly the sky-high airplane.
You are equipped with the state-of-the-art technology
To overcome whatever that comes across you.
You are a God-made plane.
You are also equipped with world's safety features,
Producing internal tremendous force to
keep you airborne.

You are a God-driven airplane, and
Every situation the airplane is going through,
Was known before the airplane was procreated.
Your wings are large enough to stand every pressure.
You do not need a data recorder.
You are one of the luxury and sophisticated planes.
Your engines produce perfect turbine to stomach storms.
Your transponder keeps you located.
Your auxiliary power unit is always perfect.
You have a perfect radar.
Your pilot crew has the best track record,
They knew things before they occurred.
No need to run before you take off.
No need to do manual check-up before you take off.
No falling from the sky.
No catastrophic failure.
Crash landing is a thing of the past, and
Your safety is hundred percent guaranteed.

4

Listen to My Heart Speaks

Take a sit on massage pallor couch.
Forget about yourself.
Forget about the root of evil.
Take off your clothes of misjudgment.
Throw away your diamond earrings of underestimation.

Lay down on the couch and close your eyes.
Listen to sweet melody.
The room is wearing fire and ice fragrance.
Let sensory adaptation take its course.
The room is made up of white and red flowers.

Let me roll up my sleeves.
Let me cry tears of joy until there is no tears in my heart.
If you could see yourself in the mirror of my heart,
You could see the true meaning of you.
Together, there is nothing impossible.

Tell me how can a man like me,
Convince a woman like you to be his queen?
How can I convince love angels to open
Heaven's gates for me and you?
How can I make you to swallow your pride?

Hey, gorgeous, remove your bracelet of
Judging a book by its cover.
If you could look at me with your heart,
You could see love sparkling within
Hey, gorgeous, just put a crown around my head.

5

Before I Let It Go

Before I bury the hatchet,
Let me get my emotions in healing process.
Let me grief to cry out my anger.
Let me adapt to a new world of sorrow.
Let me allow these tears that fill my eyes to fall down.
Let me get your motive behind your deeds.

Before I ease your conscience,
I need the gist of what really happened.
I really need transparency and confession.
I need truth and reconciliation to be done.
I need my gash to be properly taken care of.
I need to make it clear to you that I cannot just let it go like that.

Before I ease your heavy loads on your shoulder,
Do you really understand what you did to me?
Do you really understand the pain I am going through?
Do you know that heart takes time to heal when you hurt so much?
Do you know that I cannot overlook what you put me through?
Do you condemn yourself?

Before I forgive you and forget,
Bear with my velocity to a land of healing.
Before we sing the song of forgiveness,
Let my heart get mended.
Before I redress,
Cross your fingers and tell me you will not do it again.
Take my hand, now I am ready to sing along with you the song of forgiveness.

6
Comfort Zone

Poverty is a product and reward of laziness.
Poverty is for those who go
With a flow like dead fish.
Poverty is a blanket that blankets
Those who are in comfort zone.

You are poor by choice,
Not by chance.
You choose to be poor
By not thinking outside the box.
Complaining without
Acting has no use.

Get out from mediocrity.
Get out from your comfort zone.
Get out from inferiority.
Stop complaining.
Start thinking big, and
Start using your hands

Strive for success
Work like a slave.
While others are sleeping,
Push, push, push, and
Keep pressing harder.

Never allow tiredness to kick in.
Success is for those who dare to dream.

Be resilient.
Be unwavering committed goals
Be energetic.
Be hungry for success.
Don't focus on your situation
You facing now,
Focus on what is coming next,
And live your dreams.

7

Try Me

Maybe you have tried the best of the best,
And they have failed you.
Try me;
I am the best above
All the best.
I am a friend you can always count on,
Through thick and thin.

Forever and ever,
Through good and bad time,
In heat of the night,
During the day,
My love for you
Will be endless,
Unconditional and constant.
Even seasons may change,
My love for you will remain constant.

Cast your troubles,
And your tribulation to me,
Because my shoulders are broad enough
For whatever.

Let me take charge of your life

And guide you
I swear
I will not fail you.
I am the provider
And creator,
The beginning,
The end,
The first and the last.

I will make sure that
You never stand alone.
I will lead you to prosperity, and
I am ever ready.
I know you when you were a fetus.
What tomorrow has in store for you,
With me, there is nothing
Will ever stand on your way.
I am the conquer of conquerors.
Right now, I hand over to you the power of victory.
With faith, there is nothing will stand on your way.

8

Suicide

Put down that gun.
Put that poison away.
Throw away that rope.
Committing suicide
Won't solve anything.
Killing yourself
Is not an option.

Don't be a fool,
There is more to life.
Look beyond
Your challenges.
There is a good future ahead.
Move past mistakes without blaming yourself unfairly.
Strive to overcome negative thoughts and self-sabotage.

Look at you,
You are so beautiful,
Brave, and deserve better and happiness.
Live your life, and
Stop living to prove yourself to others.
You can change what you are
And become what you want to be.

It is never too late to change,
And the change is totally dependent on you,
Stop feeling sorry for yourself and work hard.
Feel able to try new or difficult things.
Never forget that
A recipe for success is pain,
Perseverance, and sweat.

Give yourself positive affirmation.
Recognize your strengths
To boost your self-esteem.
Remember, you are unique, and
Refrain from comparing yourself to others.
Foster positive self-image.
Learn to love yourself and believing in you.

Respect life
And Value it,
'Cause life is like water,
Running down the stream.
Once it's gone,
It's gone for good, and
It will never come back.

9

Talking in His Sleep with His God

It has been a fifty-thousand-mile walk towards my success.
It has been thirty years of waiting for my success,
My dear God.
Am I asking too much?
Am I too young to handle it, my dear God?

Listen to me, my son.
Things are not too hard for you,
And not too easy for you.
What you need to be is:

To be a right person,
To be at right place,
With a right person,
At a right time.

Now you are here with me.
No need to be worried.
You are now here with a right person, son.
Your success was just a prayer away.

Now you can dream impossible dreams.
You can climb unclimbed mountain.

You can sink unsinkable boat (self-righting boat).
You can also float non-floatable ship, but if you believe.

You need to put faith in you.
You are with your majesty father to guide you.
You need to believe that you are no longer a loser.
You will be now unstoppable.

As you are a unique person with unique fingerprints.
You are also having a unique gift.
It is hidden out there for you and only to find it.
You need to get up and find your hidden treasure,
Than make it happen.

10

Use Your Stumbling Block as Your Stepping Stone

Adapt to the situation you are facing as soon as possible, and
Face the reality.
See your downfall as your golden opportunity.
Never forget that God never close a door
Without opening a window, and
Every dog has its day.

Stop entertaining the situation you are in,
Or the person who put you through the situation you are in.
Stop running up and down like a headless chicken,
Since it has no use to cry for split milk and think deeply.
Accept the situation you are in and start planning for future,
Because life must go on.
Listen to the voice of righteousness inside you,
And tell yourself that you have the potential to do whatever.

Never forget that challenges are part and parcel of human
Being.
They are there to test your strength and make it stronger.
Never lose faith and hope.
Never let a stumbling block to stop your dreams to come
True.
Roll up your sleeves and put more effort until you
Become what you want to be.

11

I Will Fight Until I Lose My Head

Life, how dare you?
You are full of surprises.
You are full of twists and turns,
You are also full of challenges.
You are always looking for cowards of life,
To crown them with a crown of sorrow.

You know what, Life, you can't intimidate me.
I know what I want.
I am a go getter.
I am a winner, not a failure.
I am God's image,
I am the hero in the making.

I am not scared for the challenges.
I know our fight is neck and neck situation.
It may appear as if the world is on top of me.
You know what, Life, I am hard nut to crack, and
When the going gets tough, the tough get going.
I will never quit the fight until I am on top of the world.

I am a winner with benefit of no doubt.
I will fight you, Life, until what I visualize is

being materialize.
I am the jack of all trades.
I am the atomic bomb.
I am taller than the depth of the sea.
I am strong than iron.
I am a God-driven force.

I am man enough to face whatever.
The more you strike, the more I become more powerful.
I know what I am looking for is under thousands of
Tons of rocks.
I won't stop digging until the diamond and gold is
On the palm of my hand.
I am the core of high coping mechanism.
I won't surrender.

12
Change Your Mindset

Maybe you are touched by life ferociously,
In a way that you are now hopeless,
And you do not believe in yourself anymore.
Maybe you have been fishing for the past years,
Without a single catch.
It is never too late to change.
Change your mindset
And your way of doing things.

Stop looking for job,
And start looking for business.
Cast your net in the depth of the sea for catch.
Shake things up
To avoid getting the same results.
Change your position
To get connected to network called God, and
Start living abundance quality life.

When you are employed,
You are pursuing somebody's dreams.
When you are employed, you cannot be wealthy,
But you will be living from hand to mouth, or
You will be making ends meet.

One day, you and your qualifications,

You will retire, and your qualifications will lose value, and
Your qualifications will be not transferable to an heir,
While the business is transferable to heir and
never retired or lose value.

Salary is like an Anastasia to withstand the pain, or
Dependence producing drugs
That the employer keeps on injecting you
On monthly basis,
So that you keep on making his dream
come true.
Salary is like a swing that is giving you something to do;
However, it does not get you anywhere.

There will be no generational wealth when you are
employed.
You started from the stretch, and
Your kids have to start from the stretch like you,
Just to be able to make ends meet.
Income cannot make you wealthy,
But business and assets will, since they keep value,
Or increase over time, and
It can make you wealthy, and
It gives you a generational wealth.

13
Who Are You?

Some people pray for you.
Some, they work for you.
Some, they spend on you.
Some say you are everything.
Some say you are source of happiness.

Everybody loves you.
Everybody who has you, walks proud.
Some use you to get what they don't have.
Some people believe you are the master key.
Some people sacrifice with their lives to have you.

Some people are killing other people because of you.
Some, they get killed because of you.
Some people are looking for you 8 km under.
Some are looking for you in water.
You are magical; with you, there is nothing impossible.

You even make a world go around and round.
You envelop people with dignity.
Some say you come and go.
Some say you are the ability of matter to do work.

Some people, they choose not to sleep because of you.
Some choose to leave their loved ones because of you.

You are the password of abusing people who are desperate for you.
You are always accompanied by guns and bulletproof cars.
You are the source of crime.
Who are you really?

14

Do Not Provoke Me Because You Will Not Stomach Me

I am hard to get, but once you have me, you have me.
I rub shoulder with everyone.
I am bisexual and ready for any gender.
Once you marry me, there is no divorce.
I am warning you, if you need me, be ready for lifetime relationship.

Risk factor is my transport.
I visit more especial overexcited people who live like there is no tomorrow.
I like challenges, and who is fooling who game.
Don't claim that you are clever than me, because I will prove You wrong to the whole world.
I am warning you, if you are not ready for me, you better not propose me.
I like those who skate on thin ice.

I am a unique person and relay is my wonderful game.
I am like a secret, once you have disclosed it, is gone for good.
I am so powerful, and I can marry thousands and thousands of people.

If you want to challenge me, you better think twice.
Once my love stings you, there is no turning back.
I am rough, and I can kill you.
If you do not want to provoke me, please do not cheat.
You better introspect yourself if you do want me.
I like those people who play soccer bare-footed.
If you are focused, forget about me.
You better open your eyes because I am around.

15
My Beautiful Flower

What a beautiful flower,
Your stigma,
Your red petals are beautiful and attractive.
You look fresh and your petals are sprinkled with dew,
Your aroma smells so good,
You reward every visitor with pollen grain on their feet.

I wish I were a bee,
I am sure I was going to inherit your beauty.
Hey, you beautiful flower, would you open the petals
of your heart for me,
Let me in and smell your aroma.
Your anthers are gold and fluffy,
Your style is sexy, and your beauty makes me speechless.

For sure, you are going to bear gorgeous fruits like you.
Would you allow me to take you home?
I will be the one to make you feel all right.
Your wish will be my command.
I will make sure that you always stay beautiful.
Ooh, my beautiful flower.

16
I Will Never Quit My Fight Until I Reach My Destiny

I walk the walk,
Talk the talk.
I fight the fight.
I run the race.

I am a contender,
Not a loser.
I am proactive,
Not reactive.

I am a hard worker,
Not a lazy person.
I prescribe.
I do not transcribe.

I fight like a champion.
I sting like a beer.
I cut like a razor.
I am hotter than volcano.

I do not quit the fight
Because of a few knockouts.
Pain gives me strength,
Not to give up.

I am walking a zero
To hero walk.
No matter how hard life is,
I will never quit.

Life challenges stimulate
My high thinking capabilities.
Unfavorable condition mold me, and
I will persevere until I succeed.

17
You Need To Keep the Candles Burning through the Storm

Whatever the storm you are going through in your life,
You must know it is here,
To test your strength, not to kill you,
To shape you, mold you, and
To take you to the better heights.
When life is panel beating you,
Be resilient and take shape,
Because God will not let you be tempted
Beyond what you can bear.
You have to keep the candle burning
And fight your way out,
Even if you are going through
A muddy trail.

You have to keep the candle
Burning through the storm.
Never let tiredness to kick in,
Never let fear make you to lose focus,
'Cause the brave is not he who does not feel afraid,
But he who conquers that fear.
No matter how hard things may become

Never give up.
Keep pressing on.

You can do it.
Never give in.
Forge ahead toward the storm you are facing, and
Keep the candle burning through the storm.

The victory is calling you,
Put more effort.
Push harder like you never pushed before.
Fight life like you never fought before.
It's do or die situation,
Fight your way out,
Keep fighting tooth and nail,
The fight is neck and neck,
With your situation.
Do not let the situation you are facing
To strike while the iron is hot.
You have to keep your head up, and
Keep the candle burning through the storm.

Face the storm toe to toe,
Never let the storm to deter you.
Keep going forward against the storm.
Keep working hard like a dog, and
Never allow this storm to be a stumbling block from
Accomplishing your dreams, work one's finger to the bone and

Make every day count,
'Cause this storm will pass.
Push yourself to your limit,
'Cause where there is a will, there's a way.

Burn the candle at both ends, and
Be persistent to the end, 'cause you need
To keep the candle burning through the storm.

18
My Promise

Honey, I make this promise to you
Before the marriage officer and witness.
I write it in my heart and in your heart as well
While I am kneeling and holding your hand.
My promise to you is that
My love for you will never change,
Even if the mountain could move,
But my love for you will remain
Constant.

Even if trees may shed their leaves,
But my love for you will always be there for you.
Even if ice, iron, and
Ice cream may melt,
But my love for you will remain
Growing abundantly.
Even if milk could turn into sour milk,
But my love for you will remain in abundance,
Fresh as milk and unchanged.

Sweetheart, petals of my heart,
My most beautiful flower,
Pillar of my strength,
Integral part of my life,

I love you for who you are, and
I will do by all means in my power
To keep this promise.
I make this solemn promise
Upon my honor.

19
God's Plan with You

Sometimes, you may find things
Not going your way,
Like a cell phone without reception,
Due to that, you are pursuing
Your own plans
While God is having his plan with you.

As long as you are in pursuit of your own plans,
Not God's plans,
You will not succeed,
'Cause you are not assigned to
Accomplish that vision you are currently pursuing,
Like Jonah who was sent
To Nineveh, and he chose to go to Tarshish.

Review your dreams if nothing is working out,
'Cause you might be in pursuit of
Your own dreams against God's plan.
Your dreams must be
In touch with reality.
Use what you have
At your disposal to materialize your vision.

You cannot be a pilot when you are acrophobic.

You cannot be a skipper when you are hydrophobic.
You cannot do crops farming when you hate dirt.
You cannot be a singer when you do not have a voice.
Adjust your dreams to suit you, and
Stop biting more than you can chew.

20

Failure Is Not the End

Failure is a detour, not a dead-end,
'Cause you become a failure the moment you stop trying.
Failure offers you a second chance to plan again, and
To come back guns blazing,
Head and shoulders above the rest.
Your mental toughness and attitudes are the key,
'Cause it's all about the survival of the fittest, and
Being competitive in the market called Life.

No matter how much hardship
You may face in your life,
Never give up.
Push harder than before.
Never allow defeat to kick in;
Instead, become resilient as fudge.
The crown of unsung hero, and
Heroine is calling you,
Keep on pressing and be what you want.

Put more effort than before,
Tell yourself that failure is not an option, and
You can do it.

Push against all odds,

Never let gravitational force
Drag you down.
Forge ahead toward the victory,
Remember the legacy of unsung heroes, and
Heroine never dies.

21

My Love

Darling, to me you are a love tree
That is growing in riverbank
Of the river that is ever flowing in my heart
That makes you to stay always ever-green, and
Bear fruits throughout summer and winter.
Its fruits will never go off seasons
For me to relish them.

To me, you are my trusted bank,
Where I invest my love, my feelings, and emotions.
You always ensure that the love I invest in you,
I receive it back doubled.
I love you, and my love for you
Is deeper than the depth of the ocean and seas.

I will be your sunscreen in blazing hot days.
I will always be your fortress,
To seek refuge when the world is becoming unkind
to you.
I will try my almost best to keep you happy,
Like you have been applying,
Honey on your feelings

My love for you will never die,

My love for you is most precious
Than money, gold, diamond, and
Everything in this world.
I will be with you through
Thick and thin,
Because my home is in my heart.

My love for you is firm like tree roots.
Your beauty is like a fresh blooming flower.
In morning, sprinkled with dew
That always attracts me with floral scent like a bee.
You make me feel somnambulist.
You make me feel like a happy king.
Damn, I love you.

22

Your Attitude Will Determine Your Altitude

We are born equal,
With desire and fire burning within.
To move the mountains,
It is up to individual to keep
His/her fire of being ambitious burning.
It takes courageous person
To strive for success.

It takes somebody who knows
The difference between dreaming and
Visualizing to burn the candle at both ends.
It takes a person who goes into overdrive
To be a successful somebody and
To get cracking,
'Cause procrastination is a thief of time.

The burning desire for success
Will propel those who go an extra mile.
The burning desire will enable you to hang in there,
Until what you visualize is being materialized.
Anticipate jumping through hoops,
Because it takes blood, sweat, and tear to move the mountain.

Your attitude will determine your altitude.

The more effort you put,
The greater the reward,
'Cause it takes bending over backward
To be on top of the mountain.
Remember, it takes someone who can
Keep one's nose to the grindstone
To make the cut.

Life needs those who raise the bar for others to follow, and
Those who become head and shoulder above the rest.
The hunger and burning desire to succeed
Will keep you energized and
Ever ready to stay the course.
Work your fingers to the bone,
And reap what you sow.

Keeping the desire burning for success
Will enable you to make a comeback,
'Cause where there's a will,
There's a way to overcome any obstacle.
Those who persevere toward the end,
Will hit the jackpot, and
Be on the roll.

23
It's David versus Goliath.

You know what, Life, me and you,
We are going to be David versus Goliath.
I am not scared of you,
Bring it on.
I am always ever ready to rumble you, life.
No matter what, I am going to win this contest.
It might seem as if I'm an underdog,
But you will be caught by surprise, Life, and
You will learn the hard way that
Dynamites come in small packages.

Sometimes, size does not matter,
What matters is my determination,
Courage, and the way I do things.
Don't judge a book by its cover, Life,
'Cause I have all that it takes to defeat you.
You know what, Life, I will fight you,
Tooth and nail up until I reach my destiny.
I have faced the worse and survived.
I trust myself to handle this.
I can hear the victory calling my name.

Through unwavering commitment,
I will merge victorious.
I am going to push through pain.

You know what, Life, challenges shape me,
They don't define me.
I am going to make it through
Sweat and tears,
And be what I want to be.
I will overcome the fierce fight through determination
And live my dreams.

24
Love of My Life

I wish I were your tear drop.
To be born in your eye,
To live on your dimples, and
Die in your slime gorgeous.
Your smile could heal a thousand
Wounded soldiers.
Your beauty ignited love's spark at first sight.
Now my entire body is engulfed with your love's fire.

I love you wholeheartedly, and
I see no future without you in my life, my sunshine,
Our relationship is like the relationship
Of fungus and pine trees.
The pine trees would not live without fungus, and
Fungus would not live without pine trees.
Fungus supply pine tree with nutrients and water,
While pine trees supply fungus with food.

You are so immaculate, like peach,
My heart, that you entered into,
Is like car engine, welded together
With not bolt to open.
My heart is like an island with waterfall
That flows our love throughout the year.
Rule my heart, queen of the island;
I will be your king forever.

25

God's Praise

You are the source of life.
You are the creator,
The king of kings.
You are the president
That presides over all presidents.
You are Jehovah Rapha,
The God who heals.

You are Jehovah El Shaddai,
God Almighty.
You are Jehovah Shammah,
Jehovah is there.
You are Jehovah Shalom,
God our peace.

Jehovah Yahweh,
He brings into existence whatever exists.
Jehovah Elohim,
The true God in an honorific way.
Jehovah Adonai,
Lord and master.

You are God omnipotent,
God is all powerful
You are God omniscient,

All knowing,

God Omnipresent,
Always present everywhere.

You are Jehovah Nissi,
Lord is my banner.
You are Jehovah Tsidkenu,
The Lord who is our righteousness.
You are Jehovah Jireh,
The Lord will provide.

You are Mighty God.
You are alfa and omega.
You are everything.
You are the fortress.
You are Supreme Being.
You are majesty.

You are divine being.
You are rock of ages.
You are God the love, and
You are God the light.
You the Lord is a great God, and
A great King above all Gods.

You are Jehovah Ei Elyon,
The most high God.
You are Jehovah Qanna,
The lord that is jealous.
You are Jehovah Sabaoth,
The Lord of Hosts.

You are Jehovah Ei Olam,
The everlasting God.
You are Jehovah Mekoddishkem,
The lord who sanctifies you.
You are Jehovah Raah,
The lord my shepherd.

26
Dear Child

My child, I love inexplicably.
I will give you everything,
Though I do not have much.
I am prepared to work hard
For you to get a better education.
I will take care of you and
Nurture you.

Honor me your father, and
Your mother that your days may be long.
Respect elders, respect life,
So that it will respect you back.
Respect every human being,
So that God will remember you
When you are going through rough patch.

Be a hard worker,
'Cause laziness leads to poverty.
Sometimes, life is like a stove, and
You are like a pot.
It does not matter how hot the stove is,
The pot must keep on cooking till the food is ready,

'Cause in this world, it's about the survival of the fittest,
The pot that is not properly nurtured will melt

during cooking process.

Nurture the seed of respect
That I have planted in you.
It will bear fruits and
Add blessing to you.
Never forget to seek
Guidance from God,
To lead you to prosperity,
'Cause without him, you will be having no direction in life.

The future is in your hands.
It's up to you to make us proud as your family.
In life, there is no such a thing called smooth sailing.
It's about being resilient.
It's about being focus.
It's being dedicated.
It's about fighting tooth and nail,
Up until you live your dreams.

The future is in your hands.
It's up to you to make us proud as your family.
In life, there is no such a thing call smooth sailing,
It's about being resilient,
It's about being focus,
It's about being dedicated,
It's about fighting tooth and nail,
Up until you live your dreams.

27
Die Trying

To die trying is better
Than dying sitting on your bum,
'Cause only dead fish go with the flow.
Don't ever doubt yourself, and
Never cross the bridge until you come to it.
Sometimes in life, you must stop feeling
Sorry for yourself, and
You must die fighting like a man.

Never settle for less,
'Cause no pain no gain
Don't get intimidated,
'Cause it might not be as difficult as you think.
It's worth a shot,
'Cause tables may be turned, and
You save the day.

Sometimes in life, you have to bite the bullet, and
Tell yourself that you faced the worse
And survived.
It is better to die with your boots on.
After all, you have nothing to lose
When you soldiered on.
Nothing succeeds like success.

Life is always about taking risks,
No risk taking, no gain.
As the fortune favors the bold, and
Taking risks opens more doors
For opportunities.
Stop doubting yourself,
'Cause with faith and determination,
You will rise to the occasion.

28

A Friend in Need Should Be a Friend Indeed

Some people are like weeds into our lives,
They are there to damage us,
To compete with us for nutrients,
And to take away what they need from us.
They are in our lives, but they are not part of
Our journey and success.
They are like weeds in our lives
That need to be removed in order
To get good harvest.

It does not matter whether those weeds
Are edible or not.
Sometimes, you saw beans in your garden,
And beans germinate together with maize
That was harvested before.
You need to priorities beans and remove maize
In order for you to get a good harvest.
It is not going to be easy to get rid of useless people in
Your life, believe me.
But you have to remove them in your life
In order for you to succeed.

Sometimes in life, you need to be like a sponge,

You must able to absorb as much as you can, but

When life squeezes you,
You must release as much as possible,
Since some people are there in our lives like parasites
In a dog.
They are there to take what they need in good time.
They cannot be with the dog through bad times.
When a dog is beaten by a snake, they are quick
to leave the host.
They were there to take what they need.

Some of your friends will not go with you through
the fire,
They are just in your life to add numbers, not value.
They are in your life just to delay your blessing
and your success.
Also, to compete with you for nutrients like weeds.
Remember, a true friend is a friend in need and indeed.
You cannot be a friend with a person who is
In pursuit of different dreams,
Or the opposite of what you want to be.
Only the birds of same feather flock together.

29
Look At the World with the Eyes of a Spiritually Matured Person

It takes a spiritually matured person
To understand that we wake up
Every morning by the grace of God, not by an
alarm clock.
One day, the alarm clock will ring until
The battery dies, and
You will not wake up,
'Cause it is only God that wakes people up.

It takes a spiritually matured person
To understand that
Safety is not guaranteed in man-made things.
Therefore, pray for your safety in flights, in train, and
Moving vehicles, and
Ships, because man-made things
Are not guaranteed.

The foot does not get damaged or become shabby,
No matter how many kilometers you walk barefooted,
'Cause it's God-made.
We are changing shoes now and then,
'Cause it's man-made.
What was created by God is durable.

30
Let Us Pray for Our Leaders

Let's pray for our political leaders.
Let's pray for our traditional leaders.
Let's pray for our faith-based leaders,
To lead us with the truth.
They must not turn their blessings into a
Thorny jacket, curse to prick their people.
To do as you would be done by.

They must not forget that
Being a leader is a blessing from God,
To lead his people to prosperity.
Let's pray for leadership not to forget that
They are leading the same people like them.
Let's pray for leaders to bear in
Mind that honesty is a good policy.

They are chosen to make a
Positive impact to their people,
Not to abuse their powers,
Not to misappropriate public funds.
Leaders must bear in mind that they ought to be nice
To their people on their way up,
So that their people will be nice to them on
their way down.

31

Life Has Chapters Like a Book

Life is like an individual examination
That need not to be copied.
Since we are born with unique gifts,
We may acquire same talents,
Whoever has different gifts from God.

Life has different chapters to read.
When you are going through
A rough patch in your life,
You must not give up;
Keep reading.
There are nice chapters ahead.

Don't be despaired,
In lieu, put more effort,
Read more chapters than before.
When you are cruising through
Good and happy chapters in your life,
You must brace yourself for a winding road
To negotiate.

Life is also like a seesaw,
Sometimes, life goes your way.
Sometimes, it goes against you.

All you need to do is to roll up
Your sleeves and
Take the bull by the horns.
Keep pressing on until you find the next chapter.

32
He Is God in Every Situation We Are Facing

When you are sick,
And you have tried everything,
Nothing is working out.
Call Jehovah Rapha,
He is Jehovah who heal.
When you are being failed in life,
He is Jehovah Tsidkenu.
He is our righteousness.

He is Jehovah Shammah and
always there when you need him.
When you are tired fighting battles on your own,
And you need peace,
He is Jehovah Shalom.
When you don't know your identity,
He is the Lord, my shepherd.
The Lord who owns me.

When you need a mentor and a master
In your life,
He is Jehovah Adonai.
When you have lost direction, position,

And connection, he is omnipresent God.

He is God that is capable of being everywhere
At the same time.
He is the way when you are lost.

When you are facing tough times in your life,
And you see no way out,
He is Jehovah Jireh.
When you need supreme power
That has no limitations,

He is Omnipotence God.
He is the truth whenever you need justice.
When you are facing predicament in your life,
He is Omniscient.
God who knows everting.
When you have given up
With your life,
You are battling cancer,
No pain medication is working,
He is the life.

33
Life Is About Survival of the Fittest

I can feel the power of not giving up,
Triggering my pure instinct that is driving me
To keep fighting this harrowing moment
Where I am facing a dire predicament.
I must keep fighting to break myself free
From this situation I am facing.
No matter what, I am going to break myself free.

Giving up now is not an option,
Since it would spell the end of my life.
The only option I have is to keep fighting,
'Cause giving up means losing up everything.
I must face this situation I am facing head-on.
I am dog-tired; however, not defeated.
I will continue my fierce struggle for survival.

The sweat and the pain I am feeling right now,
Is motivating me to hang in there.
It may appear as the odds are against me,
But through endurance, courage, and
Divine intervention,
I will turn the tables
As God's image.

I am going to overcome this situation I am facing,
Dark of blue,
'Cause I am serving the living God
Who walk with us in every situation we are facing.
I will keep pressing on,
'Cause fortune favor the bold, and
God help those who help themselves.

I will continue the fierce fight
Until the end.
I am prepared to die with boots on.
I am not going to stop the fight when
I am tired, but I will stop when I am done with fighting.
I will come out victorious, and
I will relish the fruits of my hard work.

34
Every Human Being Has a Role to Play

Sugar is sweet and
Is more popular than salt;
However, sugar cannot replace salt.
No matter how popular sugar is,
You cannot use sugar instead of salt,
But you can use salt when you need salt for
Food to taste nicely.

No matter how important you think you are,
You cannot replace those people you
Viewed them as of less important than you.
So, everyone is important in this world
And is having important role to play,
Since everyone is unique,
And is assigned a unique role to play.

Every human being is inviolable and
Irreplaceable.
Let us treat one another
With mutual respect.
Let us cherish one another.
Let us not value a human being with
His/her material things,
'Cause no one in this world is living by a mistake.

35
He Is Faithful

With faith, I have been in places where I was told,
"If you enter here, there is no way out."
And have left places where people said,
"There is no way out."
Through faith and God,
I have achieved unbelievable things.

Blessed is the man who trusts in the Lord,
Whose hope is the Lord.
For he shall be as a tree planted by the waters,
And that spread out her roots by the river,
But her leaf shall be green.

You are the light of the world,
A city that is set on a hill cannot be hidden.
Neither do men light a candle and
Put it under a bushel
But on a candlestick.

As a Christian, it is very important
To know that Christianity is a lifestyle
That every Christian should live.
Christianity is not a fashion, but a lifetime commitment.
You should be living by an example, and
Be the light in the dark.

We have to worship him
For no reason,
Other than he is God.
For giving an extra day to live,
While others, they did not wake up.
For keeping us pain free,
While other are fighting for their lives.

We need to thank his mercy,
For giving us family,
For giving children that
Are not mentally and physically challenged.
For keep providing for us, and
For giving us jobs, business, shelter over our heads
et cetera.

There are many people in possession
Of the same qualification as us,
But they are unemployed.
Some of them are even
Better than us,
But the faithful God decided to give us a chance.
Let us be grateful for the blessings in our lives.

36
Life Is War

I rather be blind
Than being a sighted person with no vision.
I rather not sleep or rest
Than living a regretfully life.
I rather die empty
Than dying with unaccomplished great visions.
I rather fail thousand times
Than not trying.
I rather keep on shoot for stars
Till I get it right,
Because I know that a winner is just a loser
Who tried one more time.

I know people who never fail,
Never try.
I have to get it wrong to get it right.
I know quitting is enemy of my success, and
I will never quit.
I will be resilient as fudge, and
I will thrive on adversity.
I know life is a war, and
I have to win this war in order for me
To be a champion.
I will fight you, Life, ferociously,
No matter how many punches you are throwing at me,

I am going to soldier on.

I will come out stronger, tougher, and better,
Through fire, sweat, and pain.
I am going to win this war, and
I am not going to surrender,
I am not going to quit this fight
Or give up.
I will be a champion,
Through hard work, consistency,
Focus, and discipline.
I will change my life forever, and
My dreams will become a reality.

37
I Am Unstoppable

No gun or army can silence my voice.
No laws or oppressor
Will suppress my voice.
Even if you can make me to bite the dust,
I will rise like a phoenix from the ashes,
'Cause I am an invincible warrior and
Unstoppable.

I am a runway train,
Nobody can stop me.
I am tsunami,
Nobody can stop me.
I am the light that shines in darkness, and
The darkness can never extinguish.
I am volcano erupting,
Nobody can stop me.

I am the death,
Nobody can stop me.
When time is up,
Even if you can try to get rid of me,
My legacy will stand the taste of time.
I will rise again against all odds, and
My work will speak volume.
Nobody would erase my world record
Written in Guinness World Records.

38
The Squeaky Wheel Gets the Grease

Sometime in life you have to forget about
Your ego and swallow your pride,
'Cause only squeaky wheel gets the grease.
Let us learn to verbalize our challenges and
Predicaments to people with a heart of gold,
Who will be with us through thick and thin and
Willing to offer a shoulder to cry on.

Let us stop internalizing everything, Men.
I know we were taught not to express how we feel.
We were taught not to cry, 'cause real men does nor cry,
Whatever the case may be,
Real men do not spill the beans.
Let us stop that misconception and cry out the anger.
Let us verbalize our depression, speak out, Men, and
Seek professional help.

Talking about your problems to someone outside
of the situation
May release pent-up feelings,
May also help you to find a solution to the problem,
Rather than keeping your problems to yourself.
There are selfless spirits people out there,
Who gives someone a leg up,
As iron sharpens iron.
So, one person sharpens another.

39
Never Let Your Past Define You

Your background does not matter.
What matter the most is where you are going to,
Since you cannot change your past now.
You were born from poor family by a chance, not
by choice.
So, the ball is in your court to break the chain of poverty,
Since you cannot inherit poverty from your parents.

Never let your past to define you,
Rather let the future to define where
You are going in life,
Since you cannot live the past today.
However, you can live today now and
Future tomorrow.
What matters is what is coming next, and
The world is your oyster.

All you need to do is to
Take the bull by the horns, and
Put your nose to the grindstone.
Bear in mind that the road to success is always
Under construction and
Not straight.
It's always full of obstacles,
Potholes, and sometimes gravel.

So, you must be tough as nails and get the ball rolling.

Sometimes, you will find yourself
Up a creek without a paddle,
But never throw in the towel;
Instead, pick yourself up by your bootstrap and
Keep moving forward.
Sometimes, you will find yourself out of the
frying pan and into fire,
Never be despaired; instead, be resilient.
Remember, no retreat no surrender;
Instead, keep your eyes on the prize called success.

40
Be a Relentless Person in Life

You know what, Life,
You have met your match.
I am a professor, graduated from university of life.
I know all your tactics
Of intimidating those people who lack
Of courage to keep fighting,
Who give up fighting
Due to few stunning blows.
I will fight you, Life,
Until my whole body burns.
It does not matter how long it takes me to succeed.

I know sometimes in life, you must start from the
bottom and work hard your way up to the top,
'Cause only the hole that grow from the top to bottom.
It does not matter how tired I am,
Soaking wet with sweat, and
Excruciating pain I am feeling,
I will fight you, Life, until my hands get numb.
I don't mind you, Life, even if
You are launching a fierce attack on me.
I am not backing down an inch,
'Cause I know what I want.

I have suffered worse for wear, and

I am feeling wear and tear pains on my joints,
But I am not giving up this fight.
I know success is too expensive, and
Road leading to success is narrow,
Full of challenges, pain, suffering, and
Intimidating obstacles I must overcome.
I am going to grind it on and
Hang in there,
'Cause there's no such thing as free lunch, and
Every cloud has a silver lining.

I know you, Life, that fighting you
Is like pulling teeth,
But through being relentless,
Taking one step at time, and
Pulling out all the stops, I will make it.
I know you can't make an omelet
Without breaking few eggs.
I know things are tough right now,
But I will keep on keeping on, and
Keep my chin up until
I hit the jackpot.

41
It's Never Too Late to Bounce Back in Life

Maybe you have been
Admitting the defeat, and
You don't believe in yourself anymore
Due to disappointments and failures you went through.
You are now moving with the tide, and
You are living like there is no tomorrow.
Well, it is not too late to get up,
Dust off yourself, and
Bounce back,
'Cause life has more to offer
To those who push oneself to the limit.

Turn over a new leaf, and
Start pursuing your dreams.
The world is your oyster to be what you want to be.
The situation you were facing,
Was never meant to destroy you,
But to make you stronger like a bull,
'Cause life is rough and tough.
It may hurt you and
Inflict pain.
All you need to do is get through it.

You need to float like a butterfly and
Sting like a bee.
Never lose focus,
And let the pain and fatigue to disrupt you.
Work one's finger to the borne, and
Tell yourself that you can do it.
When life gives you lemons
Make lemonade.
Remember, the way to success
Is through overcoming many adversities.
Through grind it on.
Definitely, you will have the world at your feet.

You are tougher than you think you are, and
You can go through more than you think you can,
But if you believe in yourself and
Have the courage to succeed.
It takes sweat of one's brow to be successful,
'Cause no pain no gain.
Success is for those who endure the pain,
Who keep fighting and
Not give up.

Give it your best shot and
Never say die,
Keep fighting until the end.
The sky is the limit for those who
Reach for the stars.

Never listen to failures,

Keep fighting life and
Knock it out of the park.

Work through the pain, and
Run the race until the end.
Never let cramps and fatigue to disrupt you.
Run your own race until you cross finish line.
The price for the winner is
On the other side.
Those who cross finish line first,
Receive their reward.
Breaking the record
Deserves excellent reward.

42
Bone of My Bones And Flesh of My Flesh

This is now bone of my bones and
Flesh of my flesh.
She should be called 'woman,'
For she was taken out of me.
That is why I left my father and mother,
To be united with you, my wife, and
To become one flesh.
Your smile melts my heart and makes it skip the beat,
I also had bunch of butterflies in my tummy
As you were going down the aisle (processional).

Before our union, darling,
I was a boy, not a man, and my life was incomplete.
Now you have completed my life my better half.
As we get hitched,
You are me and I am you.
You are my other half.
I promise to love you forever,
Until death do us apart.
I have no doubt in my mind
That we are two peas in a pod.

I will love you through good
And bad times,

Through sickness and
Health.
As we tie the knot,
What is mine is yours,
What is yours is mine.
I am head over heels for you, honey, and
We are a match made in heaven, and
We are an item forever.

I love you to the moon and back,
Apple of my eye.
You take my breath away, and
I can hardly wait for you to whisper sweet nothing to my ear.
I have the hots for you, angel of my heart.
We are the true meaning of true love.

My lovey-dovey.
I wish us a happily ever after wedding and
Prosperous life together my other half.
We must always seek guidance and
Divine intervention for our marriage to be
Galvanized and to have intact family.

43
Renew Your Zeal.

When things are not
Going your way
After trying everything couple of times,
You become demoralized,
Demotivated, and be deterred,
'Cause sometimes in life, you are like fire
That need to be stocked in order for it to burn higher.

Like every tool
Becomes blunt and
Every machine needs
To be serviced and
To be well oiled.
Every equipment needs
Restoration.

Sometimes as human beings,
We need to be rejuvenated
With motivation to renew our zeal and
To restore hope to make a comeback.
Be hungry for success again,
In order for you to get back again and
Make wonders.

Run smoothly and efficiently,

Like a well-oiled machine.

Cut like sharpened knife.
Start a new life and
Be as fresh as a daisy.
Burn like oiled lamp and
Live your dreams.

44
Vicious Apex Predator

You are an unwelcome guest
Who uninvitedly visit the poor,
Rich, and wealthy people.
Young and old,
Ill and healthy human beings.
You leave your visitors shattered and
In agony with pain.

You keep on ambushing and
Stealing our loved ones.
You sting young and old,
Poor, rich, and wealthy.
You aren't willing even
To accept bribes or
Delay your visit.
You are always punctual and disciplined.

You ambush
And viciously attack our loved ones,
Leaving every family member devastated,
Hopeless, and defeated.
You are inferno that is
Consuming everything that come across your path.
You hate peace and harmony.
You are a heartless thief that is

Even changing our marital status.
You are an apex predator
With immense appetite.
You ambush and crown every
Family with a crown of sorrow.
You pounce on your prey,
Bite, and you even crush their bones.

Your visit cause pandemonium and
Rip havoc to the families.
You reward every family member and friends
With souvenirs of grief and mourning.
You are the bridge that connects
The world to other side.
You strike faster than a falcon.

45
Be Yourself No Matter What

Maybe you are facing difficulties in your life and
You are indebted.
You are no longer able to service your debt,
'Cause you chose to impress your peers
At your own expense, and
You succumbed to peer pressure,
Just to prove a point.

Some people are stuck in drugs and
There is no way out due to addiction and peer pressure.
Some are driving big flashy cars they cannot afford, and
They don't enjoy just to impress their peers.
Some are alcoholic due to peer pressure.
Some have committed crimes, and
They have criminal records through peer pressure.

Say no to peer pressure,
Stop being gullible.
Stop pretending.
Stop moving with the tide,
'Cause you might regret.
Resist the temptation and
Stand your ground.

Never ever let other people

To take charge of your life.
Stay focused and
Draw the line.
Brake away from the pack and you will not regret.
Don't be a follower, be a leader.
Than skating on the thin ice.

Be yourself no matter what, and
Never let peer pressure to highjack your future.
Never let peer pressure to possess you.
Never let peer pressure to divert your success.
Don't be afraid to stand out from the crowd,
Never bow to peer pressure, and
Just leave your peers.

46
Fight the Good Fight

Blessed are thou,
Simon, son of Jonah.
For flesh and blood hath not reveal
It unto you,
But my father which is in heaven.

Upon this rock, I will build my church, and
The gates of hell shall not prevail against it.
I will give unto the keys of kingdom of heaven, and
Whatsoever you shalt bind on earth shall be bound,
In be bound in heaven.

Not everyone that saith unto me,
Lord, Lord, shall enter into the kingdom of heaven,
But he that do will of my father which is in heaven.
Many will say to me in that day,
"Lord, Lord, have we not prophesied in your name?

And in your name have cast out devilish?
And in your name done many wonderful works?"
And then I will profess unto them,
"I never knew you,
Depart from me.
Ye that work iniquity."

I have fought a good fight,
I have finished my course,
I have kept the faith,
Henceforth, there is laid up for me,
A crown of righteousness.

Being a Christian without meeting
Required standard,
Without fighting a good fight,
Without finishing the course,
Is not good enough to meet
The criteria to enter the kingdom of heaven.

For the fact that there is a key of kingdom of
Heaven.
It is crystal clear that space of kingdom of
Heaven is strictly reserved for those who
Do God's will.

Not everyone that say Lord, Lord,
Shall enter into the kingdom of heaven.
Saying, Lord, Lord, is not good enough.
Going to church every day is not enough.
The crown is for those who finish the course and
Who kept the faith.

47
You Swept Me of My Feet.

Hey, beautiful.
You are so pretty as a picture, and
You look drop-dead gorgeous in your red dress.
You smell so good.
Your soft and silky skin make me weak at the knees.
Your beauty is like of a blooming red rose in the morning.
Your smile gorgeous short a cupid's arrow,
Straight to my heart.

I just want to let you know that
You swept me off my feet
The first time I laid my eyes on you.
Now, I can't help it.
I think you have hang the moon in the sky.
I am really falling in love with you, and
I only have eyes for you my chocolate granules, and
I love you wholeheartedly.

You stole my heart, and
You left me crazy in love.
I love you from the bottom of my heart.
You make my heart to skip a beat and
Forget how to breathe.
My chest emerges a love spring
That flows down to my heart and

Fills up my heart with endless love.

I just want to let you know that
I love you, and your beautiful eyes
Make my heart melt.
You are the light of my life, and
I love you to death.
You are the air that I breathe.
You set my heart on fire,
Now I am burning of your love.

I wish I were your dress,
To envelop your body tightly.
I wish I were your bed that you sleep in
All night long.
I wish I were your smart watch
To monitor your heart beats.
Just give me a chance to prove
That I am madly in love with you.

48
Love Serpent

You are sleek, agile,
And beautiful serpent
That is armed with sharp fangs of love.
You are highly aggressive.
You are deadly lover serpent.
You are known for your large size.
You are known for quickness
And extremely potent venom.

You ambush
And strike unexpectedly.
You inject your neurotoxic venom
That cause paralysis to your victim.
You are happy to see your victim
Suffocating and becoming weak until
Their vital organs shut down and
Your victim dies in agony.

Kiss me with your kiss of death,
'Cause I am slowly dying inside of your love.
My love for you is like cancer in my heart
That is keeping my heart bleeding profusely,
While you are playing a hard-to-get game with heart.
Your venom is killing me inside,
And there is no anti-venom that may reverse
Your love venom.

49
Rise Up Against Gravitational Force

Let them badmouth you,
Let them call your names,
Let them gossip about you,
Let them call you stupid, failure, and a fool.
Don't confront or argue with them,
'Cause you will be wasting your time
By trying to prove a point, 'cause what they are saying
About you, will not change who you are.

You cannot become a fool
Simply because they call you a fool.
You cannot become a loser
Simply because they call you a loser.
What they are saying about you, will not hurt you
Without your concern.
But the pain you will be feeling, will be self-induced
By sensitizing what they have been saying to you.

Remember, water is meant
To keep the boat afloat when remaining outside the boat.
Never let water inside your boat; call your mind,
Let the haters smack you,
'Cause your success makes them green with envy.
Mind you, a fear or anxiety toward moving

vehicle makes a dog buck.

For the fact that empty vessels are now making noise,
That means you are doing something.

Keep working harder while they are gossiping about you.
Haters going to hate; however, never allow them
to disrupt you.
Fly against the wind like an eagle.
Fly to fierce winds and
Use the storm current to rise higher.
Remember that anyone who is seeking
To do evil against believer, will fail.
Rise to the occasion,
'Cause success is a sweet revenge.

50
Success

My name is success.
I am like a cake.
I am sweet.
I am up for grabs.
You can cut me as you like,
Provided you have the fighting spirit.

I am within the reach,
Only to focus people.
It does not matter whether you are tall,
Short,
Big or small,
Young or old.

I am attainable.
Catch me if you can.
If you are not focused,
Resilient, and you do not
Believe in yourself,
Forget about me.

I rub shoulders
With go getters,
Day dreamers,
Risk takers,

Who do not take no
For an answer.

I like those who try and
Keep trying till
They get it right.
I like those who give their blood,
Sweat, and tears in order for them to succeed.
I like the tried and tested ones.

Catch me if you can,
I am across winding road,
With potholes called obstacles.
I play hard to get to lazy people.
Work like a slave if you want me.
Stop working when you are done, not when are tired.

51
My Paradise

You are my most beautiful place.
My place of contentment.
My land of luxury and
Fulfilment, containing everlasting bliss.
My comfortable and cozy atmosphere.
Your beach has crystal clear water and
Gently lapping waves.
My place of tranquility.

My popular and stunning holiday destination.
You are an inimitable place.
You are the quintessential destination.
You afford superlative ecotourism beach.
You are island paradise that offers
The world beautiful beaches
That has coral reefs.
You are my ecstasy.

You are my heaven on earth and
A luminous island that promises escapism.
You are my holiday destination that lives up to hype.
Your food is divine and out of this world.
Your breathtaking beauty waterfalls that
Pouring water that splashing spray
Mist of droplets that create rainbow.

You are captivating island that stole my heart.
You are my soothing island.
You are my serene paradise.
You are my sanctuary that is protecting me from the sun.
You are a place where imaginations meet reality.
You are my place of exceptional happiness.
You are my relaxing destination.

You are my beautiful paradise
Where comfort, exoticism, modernity, and
Diversity meets.
My ultimate destination for summer fun, and
Adventure where I enjoy endless trills and excitement.
These magnificent natural wonders lead
To a truly unforgettable experience, my heaven on earth.

52
Shooting Star

Shoot the sky, shooting star.
Let the lucky ones make wishes.
Shoot the sky, symbol of good luck.
Shoot the sky, symbol of magical abilities.
Shoot the sky, beacon of hope.
Shoot the sky, symbol of positive change.
Shoot the sky, symbol of love and victory.
Make their wishes to come true.
Shoot the sky, glowing streak of light
That energize the dreamers.
Shoot the sky, star that shoot
Once in a blue moon.
Open sesame the star of endless possibilities and
Let everyone's wishes to become true.

53
Procrastination Is a Thief of Time.

I am going to start when time is right.
I am going to start tomorrow.
I am waiting for the right moment.
I am going to kick-start my business
When I have enough money;
Colorful excuses, one after another.
What if the right moment you are waiting
For will never come?
What if tomorrow never comes?
What if the perfect moment never comes?

Stop making colorful excuses and
Start changing your life right now, 'cause there's
No time like present.
Never let the opportunity pass you by,
Because you snooze, you lose.
Tell yourself that I have to do this right now,
It's now or never.
Do things at the drop of a hat,
'Cause opportunity comes once in a blue moon.
Never wait for the perfect moment,
Because it will never come.

There will be no right moment that will be

Right as rain in your life.

Tell yourself that I will dive in and
Do my best come rain or shine.
Remember, success will cost you
An arm and a leg, and
Success is not a dime a dozen.
Sometimes, you will find yourself
Barking up the wrong tree and
Finding your effort going down in flames.

Never throw in the towel.
Stick to your guns and refuse to compromise.
Go back to the drawing board and plan again.
Get your act together and avoid cutting corners.
Get ready to take the bull by the horns and
Rip off the Band-aid.
Get the ball rolling,
Because action speaks louder than words.
Put your nose to the grindstone and
Hit the nail on the head.

Keep your fingers crossed,
Put more effort and you will hit a homerunning.
Never procrastinate, because early bird catches the worm.
Never ever talk about your business ideas
To anyone because they will steal them and
You will be caught napping.
If you can go and stand in front of the mirror,
Wearing the same cloths as before, you see no change,
Up until you change first before going to mirror,

Then you will see change.

So, if you want change in your life and
Different results,
Turn over a new leaf.
Are you tired of the life you are living right now,
Yet you are sitting on your bums doing nothing?
Wake up and smell the coffee.
Stop whining while you are not doing
A thing to change
your life.
Shake things up; although, it is not going to be
Walking in the park.

Getting your ideas in action is uphill battle,
But when you are resolute and courageous,
Nothing will ever stand in your way.
Remember, success is for those who burn
The midnight oil.
Some changes will make you feel like a fish
Out of water for a while up until you get used to it.
Keep on pressing because comfort zone
Is the enemy for success.
Go to great lengths.

54
Take Eagle's Mentality Into Action.

I am beautiful and powerful.
I am ambitious, disciplined, and energetic.
I am having immense appetite for success.
I believe in me, and I am proud of myself as peacock.
I believe that I was born to succeed.
I am going to adopt the eagle's mentality
Of thriving on adversities.
I know it is a mentality of an eagle
That makes it to be fearless, successful, and
To become the king of the sky.

So, I am going to employ evolving and
Formidable hunting strategy of an eagle to succeed.
I am going to show you, Life, what I am made of and
What I am capable of.
I am going to prove you, Life, that my mentality
Will keep me going until I win.
I am going to put a brave face on upcoming difficult situation,
Forge ahead, and going stronger and stronger,
'Cause I am made up of dominance, wisdom,
Discipline, and victory.
I don't care even if I suffer on my way to success,
'Cause there is no easy way to the top.

I have to suffer in order for me to succeed and
Relish the fruits of my hard work forever.
I am making commitment with success right now,
As long as I live, I am going strive for great heights.
As it is a nature of the eagle to hunt all day long.
From now on, it will be my nature to strive
For greater heights of success against all odds.
I am going to hit the ground, running and
Putting muscles on it,
'Cause it takes braking one's back in order
To be successful.
I am all way out,
Nothing will stand on my way.

Come what may,
I will buckle down.
No matter what hardship I may face,
I will bear down, and
I am going to knuckle down.
It's either sink or swim; I am going to venture into uncharted waters and win.

I am going to take the ball and run with it.
I will toil away until I live my dreams.
Nothing will stop me.
No matter what, I will win.
No matter how painful is the process
It will be,
I am going to paddle one's canoe,
'Cause success is for those who swim

Against the tide, and
As too many cooks spoil the broth.

I am going to work like a dog,
All the way to the top.
I am going to keep one's eye on the ball, and
I am not going to let this opportunity to sleep away.
I will keep on working hard until I succeed.

55
Never Lose the Moon While Counting the Stars

Sometimes, we lose most important
People in our lives
While we are being preoccupied and
Channeling our attention and
Energy to wrong people.
Its real cut is like a knife to lose
The apple of your eye, while
We are focusing on a wolf in sheep's clothing
That do not value us
As our immediate family does.

It is very painful to lose the moon
While counting the stars,
'Cause the stars will be not with you when life
Take you out of the frying pan and into fire, while
Your family will be all in the same boat with you.
A family is very close-knit and the ties that bind
Our family together remains strong no matter what.
The family is the precious gift of them all.
Nobody will ever be so special and
Be most valuable than our immediate families.

Your family will be standing by you
Being a shoulder to cry on.
Come what may,

Your family will be a shoulder to lean on.

Your family will be the first and
The last line of defense in time of need,
As blood runs thicker than water.
Your family will be the first to arrive and
Be the last to leave in time of need,
'Cause blood is thicker than water.

When you are a married man,
You should be a family man.
Your wife comes first,
Your kids second,
Your extended family third, and
Your friends and colleagues last.
Your wife will be with you through thick and thin,
'Cause family ties are the ties that bind.
Your wife will be the one to
Close your eyes for the last time.

Wives, submit yourselves to your own
Husbands as you do to the Lord.
For the husband is the head of the wife,
As Christ is the head of the church.
Husbands, loves you, wives,
Just as Christ love the church and
Gave himself up for her.
As a married woman your husband comes
First before everything and
Your friends last.

56
A Healthy Body Is a Healthy Mind

I am overweight or obese
That expose me to a health risk.
My doctors recommended that I must start
Losing weight
To get rid of junk food,
To exercise regularly and
To start living a healthy lifestyle.
A dietician also recommended me
To start diet program.

It's hard to kick the habit.
Exercising is too strenuous and painful.
I have no time to start exercising and
Preparing healthy food.
I will start tomorrow
To exercise and eat well.
I have started exercising,
But it's very hard.
My whole body is hurting.

Excuses and excuses after one another.
It is possible to live a healthy lifestyle and
Quit cold turkey of eating junk food.
All you need to do first,

Is to weigh the pros and cons and
Implications of the decision you are about to take.
Make an informed decision,
Start eating healthy, and
Start exercising.

It's not going to be easy, trust me.
But never give up on yourself.
The best thing to do is to start and
Stick to your guns.
Do it over and over, and
Don't look back.
You will not regret it,
'Cause the stakes are high and
It's either do or die.

Just imagine yourself,
You have to check your blood sugar
Every day.
You have to inject yourself with insulin daily.
Your life to depend on chronic medications.

You have to do surgeries in order for you
To lose weight 'cause
You cannot do it yourself.

You know what, you can do it.
It is in your mind.

Start exercising step by step
As you get used to it.

Push yourself to the limit.
Defeat the urge of junk food cravings.
Sticking on diet programs.
Exercise regularly.
Remember, no pain no gain.

Love yourself,
Eat healthy food,
Stay fit as a fiddle.
Do periodical check-ups,
'Cause prevention is better than cure.
Drink water and eat fruits,
'Cause an apple a day keeps
The doctor away.

Avoid stress
To improve your life span.
Remember, laughter is the best medicine.
Stay positive in life.
Avoid everything that will
Make you to lose self-esteem.
Burn off tummy fat and weight
To stay healthy.
Be always ready to take new challenges by the storm.

57
Island of Love

The king who rule the island is love.
A place where true love exists.
A place where true lovers reside.
A place where the rivers flow love.
A place where devoted partners love each other to death.
A place where couples whisper sweet nothings.
A place where doves are doing
A love poetry reading.

A place where its beautiful waterfall
Is cascading love.
A place where the victims of Cupid's arrow
Are falling in love.
A place where valentine's day
Is always celebrated.
A place of the most luxurious chocolate,
Honey, and sweet rose sparkling wine.

A place where lovey-dovey couples
Walk on footpaths made up of red and
White rose's petals.
A place where only romantic songs
Are played.
A place of endless bliss.
A place where rose's aroma is

Hypnotizing to everyone.

A place of endless seduction and cuddling.
A place where Hummingbirds are
Blowing saxophones that are made up of roses.
A place where couples are always happy like a kid in candy store.
A place where couples lock their red love heart-shape
Interlocked padlocks on the fence
That is engraved with couple's name,
Symbolizing their true love and lifetime commitment.

58
Autobiography

You are *crème de la crème*,
You are slick, and flashy.
You come with bells and whistles.
You are the true meaning of unwavering
Commitment to luxury.
You are the true piece of art of clever engineering.

Your designers pushed the boundaries and
They always champion a breathtaking modernity.
You are iconic symbol of British engineering.
You symbolize commitment to precision and quality.
Your comfortable sits sing lullaby song to its passengers.
Your pop-up door handles, and soft close is in another level.

You are an attractive seven-sitter beast that
Armed with state-of-the-art technology.
You are magnificent.
Your beauty is out this world.
You are the masterpiece and
Heaven on wheel.

59
All That Glitters Is Not Gold

Everything is lawful for me,
But not everything is beneficial.
Everything is lawful for me,
But I will not let myself be dominate by anything,
'Cause life is like a buffet dinner table
With wide variety of food,
Where you need to eat only
What you need and
Not what you want

Everything is lawful for me,
But not everything is beneficial.
Everything is lawful for me,
But I will not let myself be dominated by anything,
'Cause other things are legally correct
But morally incorrect.
Other things are legally incorrect
But morally correct.

Everything is lawful for me,
But not everything is beneficial.
Everything is lawful for me,
But I will not let myself be dominated by anything.
As we are living in a world where
People are living like there's

No tomorrow and
Goes where wind blows.

Everything is lawful for me,
But not everything is beneficial.
Everything is lawful for me,
But I will not let myself be dominated by anything
As we are living in a world where people
Love money more than their lives.
It is true that money is important
But it is not everything.

It is very important to stay focus
And not be disrupted by peer pressure.
It is paramount important to weight
Pros and cons before taking a decision,
'Cause all that glitters is not gold.
Be yourself no matter what,
'Cause everything is lawful for me,
But not everything is beneficial.

60
It's a Brand-New Day to Keep On Trying.

It's a brand-new day
To start afresh and
Keep moving toward my success.
It does not matter how many times I got defeated,
'Cause defeat is temporal and
Every setback is an opportunity for me to learn.
I am starting this day with a bang and
Ready to break new ground.
I feel like I am on cloud nine and
To start a day with positive thoughts.

It's a brand-new day
To break free from the past and
To push forward in life.
I am full of energy, and
I am in a happy mood to turn the page.
I am eager beaver.
I am going to try by all means,
To be on the right track,
'Cause I cannot give up on
My dreams just like that.

It's a brand-new day

For me to keep going toward my success.
No matter how painful the process is,
I will be tough as nail and fight through the pain.
I am bright-eyed and bushy-tailed and
Ready to fling myself into turning myself around for better.
Trust me.
No matter what adversity I may face,
I will keep moving forward.

I know that I must stand up toe to toe
Against myriad of challenges in order for
Me to be successful.
I have to take initiative to change my life,
'Cause every man is for himself.
I am prepared to great lengths,
In order for me to achieve my success.
I hitch my wagon to a star, and
Nothing will stop me from achieving my goals,
No matter what, I am going to hit the jackpot.

61
Success Cost An Arm and Leg

Life is tough out there,
It needs resilient people
Who fall and fail but able
To bounce back.
Who pick themselves up by
Their bootstraps and
Able to rise from the ashes.
It needs uncommon people
Who are focused and
Not deterred by danger or pain.

I believe that I am that person.
I am a unique person and
Extraordinary person
With extraordinary talent.
I stand head and shoulders above
The ordinary people.
As the space of ordinary people is too overcrowded.
I believe I was born to make wonders.
I believe that I can be what I want to be in life, and
I have all what it takes to be successful.

I have a mental toughness and endurance
To bite the bullet and
To weather the storm.

My mental endurance is going to enables me

To go to overdrive, 'cause it takes someone
Who is strong as a rock to accomplish great things.
It takes actions and self-discipline
To move the mountains.
Come hell or high water,
I am going to live up to my expectations.

I am a go getter and
Prepared to go an extra mile
In order for me to succeed.
I am going to stay the course
And forge ahead against all odds.
Come what may,
I will soldier on and
Keep pressing on against adversity.
I will go all out in order for me to succeed and
Live my dreams.

62
Love and Marriage of Now Days

We are living in a world,
Where true love is scarce.
Where most of people are driven by lust
Than true love.
Where people are falling in love
For wrong reasons.
Some people enter into relationships,
Hurt from previous relationships,
With an aim to revenge.

Some people are falling in love,
'Cause there are after material things
Or they love conditionally.
Most marriages are like public toilets
These days,
Where you find those who are married,
Want to move out.
While those who are not married,
Want to get in.

The divorce rate is high these days, and
It is crystal clear that the love seed
Fell among the thorns called obstacles and
The thorns sprung and choked it,
'Cause couples failed to nurture it and

To eliminate challenges that pose
Risk to the growth of love seed.
As a result, love seed was outgrown.

Some couples let comfort zone to kick in to
Their marriage.
Where they forget to stay competitive and
Always advertise themselves to their partners.
Every couple should strive to stay appetizing as possible
To their partners.
Couples should strive to maintain their body physique
To maintain their personal hygiene and
Continue smelling nice.

Some couples are very lucky
To have mental toughness and
Attitude to outgrow challenges
In their relationship.
They stick together, fight together
Through thick and thin, and
Their true love fire consumes every
Obstacle that comes across it,
'Cause true love conquers all.

63
Thin Line Between Winning and Failing.

We are born empty like a blank slate,
Ready for everything like water.
When you add orange juice to water,
Water becomes an orange juice.
When you add apple juice to water,
Water becomes an apple juice.

When self-discovery takes place
During socialization, it's when a human being
View him/herself as shy and inferior to others,
Incapable of fighting until they get what they want.
Some believe that fortune favors the brave, and
They believe that they have all what it takes to accomplish their dreams.

It's up to individual to view him/herself as a failure and
Incapable person, and
That is only thin line that separates the winners and failures.
Winners know that it's only over when you give up.
We only fail when we allow ourselves to fail.
We all quit when we allow ourselves to quit.

Tell yourself that you are a winner, and
You were born to win.

Even if you fall, you are going to pick yourself up.
Keep pressing on against all odds.

Keep on pushing to the end,
Until you have the world at your feet.

Never doubt yourself or
Look down on yourself.
You have all what it takes to win.
All you need is to face your challenges head on,
Stop at nothing, and
Keep fighting until you live your dreams.

64
Choose Your Friends Carefully.

Make friends with people who speak the same language,
'Cause friends have a strong influence on ourselves.
As the saying goes, "Show me your friends and
I will show you your future." And
The birds of same feathers must flock together
Through thick and thin.

Make friends with peers of same caliber as you,
'Cause one rotten potato may spoils the entire bag.
Ensure that your friendship is based on principles, and
Never let your friends to break your principles.
True friends should have each other's back and
Bury the hatchet after a conflict.

True friends should be in same boat with you,
Ride or die,
As a friend in need is a friend indeed.
True friends should be as thick thieves, and
Be on the same wavelength as you and
Honest to each other.

True friends should give you a leg up and
Be pillars of each other's strength.
Be a wind beneath each other's wing,
Helping each other to reach great heights,
Taking each other under their wings,
As iron sharpens iron.

65
Keep On Trying Till Something Happen

Its undeniable that I am facing sticky situation right
Now, and I have been trying couple of times
To change my life for better;
However, nothing is working out.
It seems as if the wheel is not turning at all;
However, I don't mind, 'cause I know that
Life is a marathon, not a sprint.

I know that most successful people started
With humble beginning and
They have made it against tall order.
I know very well that good things come to
Those who wait and keep on trying.
I am going to keep on trying slow and steady till I
Turn a corner, 'cause a setback is a setup for comeback.

Sometimes in life, you need to be patient and
Be persistent like a fisherman.
A fisherman keeps on fishing even if fishes are not biting,
And remain as cool as cucumber.
Fisherman keep baiting
Even if he is not caching a thing.
A fisherman even fights a big fish more than an hour.

I am going to keep on
Taking the fight,
And fight back against the adversity.
It's been a tough row to hoe,
But I am not giving up,
'Cause life has no reverse gear.
I will keep on trying till something happen.

66
Never Let Fear to Deter You

A child can't learn how to walk
If allow a fear of falling,
'Cause a child falls several times before mastering it.
A child cannot learn running
If allow basophobia;
However, due to courage and instinct to learn, a child conquers all.

You cannot be successful in life
When you are afraid of taking risks and falling,
'Cause success is for those who able to land on their feet and
Recover well after setbacks.
You cannot be successful when you are afraid of pains,
'Cause no pain no gain, and
Pain is nothing when you have courage to win.

Success is for those who force themselves
To move forward against all odds.
Success is crown worn by champions
After winning fierce fighting,
'Cause it takes fighting like cats and dogs and
Fighting fire with fire to their opponent and emerges victorious.
You cannot fight a fierce fight and come out unscathed.

Success is for those who continue working hard and diligently
Working their fingers to the bone.
Success is reserved for those not deterred by danger.

Success is for those who are prepared to put in their blood,
Sweat, and tears to accomplish their dreams.
Even if they fall, they manage to rise from ashes and
Stay ahead of the games.

67
Turn Your Tragedy Into Your Triumph

Whatever tragedy you come across in life,
It's not meant to kill you; however, to test your strength,
Firmness of your faith, and
To make you stronger.
Face your tragedy toe to toe.
Accept and adapt it as soon as possible,
'Cause life has to go on.
Focusing on your tragedy, and
Feeling down in the dumps
Will be like flogging a dead horse and
Hurting yourself even further.

Even if you can cry,
Laugh about your situation,
Nothing is going to change the status quo since
It has no use to cry over spilt milk.
It is wise to come to terms with your tragedy, and
Be strong mentally and be courageous.
Resist tripping, falling, and loosing focus on your triumph.
Create positive growth by capitalizing on adversities, and
Turn you stumbling block into steppingstone.
Never give up on yourself,
'Cause every cloud has a silver lining.

Remember, everything happen for a reason in our lives, and
Remember that God will never close the door without
Opening another.
Work you fingers to the bone
No matter how difficult the situation is.

Never give up.
Keep on going, and keep on trying.
Stay the course.
Change the narrative,
Rewrite your own history, and
Rise like a phoenix from the ashes.

68
Walk the Talk

Success is about walking the talk,
Not about what you say or what you are capable of.
Success is about executing plan of action,
Turning your vision into action, and
Turning your vision into reality.
You must seize the day and
Make the most of each moment count,
'Cause life waits for nobody.

Aim high and work yourself to the limits.
Keep on chasing your dreams and
Strive for success every moment.
Rise and shine and
Burn the midnight oil.
Put your nose to grindstone.
No matter how difficult the situation is, don't be distracted.
Give it your all and be courageous.

Stay the course come what may.
Push the envelope in order for you to achieve
Something extraordinary.
Never say never.
No matter what, remain resilient.

Find the silver lining no matter how hard things may be.

Hang in there and
Keep believing in yourself.

Stay positive and
Turn lemons into lemonade.
Don't look back and
Keep on going forward against all odds.
Put all your strength to bear,
In order for you to achieve your dreams.
Follow your heart and
Make it happen.

69
We Will Reap What We Sow

Whatever we do we need to do it with a greater care,
'Cause whatever we do is under CCTV surveillance, and
God is watching us in his Closed-Circuit Television room, and
The footage of our actions will be played on judgment day,
And we will be answerable for our actions.

Everyone will reap what he/she sow and,
As you know, you cannot sow lemon tree and reap oranges.
Your actions will determine your destination.
It is wise to be loyal to yourself than
Pretending to be loyal to other people while you are not.

Stay true to yourself and be frank,
'Cause we are under CCTV surveillance, and
We will be held accountable for our actions.
Those who do God's will, their bodies that are sown
perishable, are raised imperishable.

There will be a pay day for our deeds.
We will be prosecuted for our actions.
During the judgement day,
Stimulus-centered scale will be used
To weigh our bad deeds and good deeds.

70
United We Stand

If we can put our differences aside and
Rally behind one another to rebuild and help one another,
As we do when our national teams are playing and
When there is national disaster, we can do more and
Change the world to be worth of living.

If we can come together as one,
Strengthened in our numbers, we can overcome any obstacle.
Change the world for better,
'Cause together we can make a difference since
Collaboration is the key.

When we are working together,
All hands on deck, we become unstoppable and indestructible,
Like burning firewood that are burning together.
We can overcome all social ills in our society,
'Cause united we stand, divided we fall.

Working hand and glove unite us irrespective of our skin color and foster building bridges, not walls.
In the midst of this national disaster,
We all know that we are one for all, all for one and
We will turn the tide.

71
Mind Your Tongue.

Tongue is like a double-edge sword.
It is a small organ, yet it can heal or hurt someone.
It can build or destroy someone.
Be careful what you say and
How you say it.
You rather bite your tongue than
Putting your foot in your mouth.

Tongue is like a matchstick, and
It is small, yet it can burn down
The whole wild world.
Giving the rough edge of your tongue
May cause emotional trauma and
Leave someone with emotional scars.
It is wise to think harder before you speak.

Learn to hold your tongue when you are angry,
To avoid saying something you will regret later,
'Cause you can't unring a bell.
Tongue-lashing inflicts pain and
Shows disrespect, whilst keeping a civil tongue
Promote mutual respect.
Desist from setting your tongue wagging because it fosters disunity.

72
You Hold Me Up

You became a source of encouragement,
Whilst my life was hitting a rock bottom.
You hold me up, and you did not let me fall.
You stood by my side in dire straits.
You have offered me a helping hand, my brother for life.
That's what brothers are for.

Brother for life become each other's
Pillar of strength.
Offer a crutch for each other to lean on.
Be lifeline during challenging times,
Giving each other a leg up and
Extending a helping hand.

I will return the favor since I am back on my feet again,
Since you scratch my back and I will scratch yours,
I will be your shoulder when you cry.
I will go bat for you against the hatters,
I will be a rock in times of trouble,
'Cause one hand washes the other, my brother for life.

You always have a selfless spirit,
Like Mother Teresa.
Never let the situation to change
Your heart of gold, my brother for life.
I am following suit, making positive impact in society, and
Big ups, my brother for life.

73
Never Play With Fire

Don't be a fool and,
Skate on thin ice,
'Cause drugs will ruin your life and turn it upside down.
You will become a slave of keep on feeding monkey.
In drugs, there is no way out.
Don't try tasting illicitly drugs, 'cause
You will be hooked and
End up in the throes of addiction.
You batter refrain from playing with fire.

Complete abstain from illicitly drugs,
'Cause it will destroy your life and
Bury you alive.
Watch your steps, 'cause illicit drugs
Are packed with dependence-producing substance.
Be warned that illicit drugs are like neurotoxic venom.
They paralyze you and take charge of your life.
You better keep your head down,
'Cause quitting illicit drugs is like finding a need in a haystack.

Illicit drugs are like a spider web,
Once you are entangled,
You cannot set yourself free.
You will be tossing and turning on the spider web.

You will be fiending for illicit drugs, 'cause
There is no turning back.
Illicit drugs will be turning your life upside down, so
Abstain from drugs because there will be no peace in your life.

74
Never Let Jealousy Thrive in You.

Lending someone a hand
Is the right thing to do.
To be inspired and motivated by other people's success
Is the key, 'cause jealousy prevents you from growing and
Learning from others.
Jealousy can destroy your happiness.
Jealousy is like a cancer that thrive on you like parasitic plant
That cause harm to you and
Inflicts pain when others prosper.

It can create unhealthy and unnecessary competition with others.
Never let green-eyed monster to make you a self-centered person.
Never let jealousy to abduct and possess you and
Make you to become green with envy against the achievers.
Never bow to pressure to keep up with the Joneses;
Instead, be yourself and pursue your own ends and
Seek advice from successful people.

Desist from fanning the flames,
'Cause it will backfire.
Never eat your heart out; instead,
Celebrate other people's success.

Never cast in a bad light to someone;
Instead, leap into flame.
Refrain from cutting down other people to size,
Badmouthing them instead, build bridges rather than walls.
Refrain from a covetous eye, 'cause every god has its day.

73
Children are Like Seeds in the Seed Bank

Children are the future of each country,
Like seeds in the seed bank.
Without them, there is no future.
We must nurture them well,
With norms and values and
Take them under our wings.
We must handle them with care,
Like seeds in the seed bank, 'cause once the entire
Seeds are damaged in the seed bank,
There will be no future of the nation.

We must lead them by examples, 'cause
What you do to your kids will follow suit.
Monkey see, monkey do.
Let us ensure that kids learn something at mother's knee.
Let us shower them with love, and
We must not give them a cold shoulder, 'cause
They need to spend quality time with us.
We must walk on eggshells around them,
Bearing in mind that spare the rod and spoil the child.
We must grease their wheels.

Let us be careful on what we say, 'cause
Little pitchers have big ears.

Let us show them that they are our sunshine,
Pride, and joy.
Let us mentor them and bear in mind that
It takes a village to raise the child.

We must encourage them to speak up,
'Cause shy brains get nowt.
Train up a child in the way he should go, and
When he is old, he will not depart from it.

74
Life Is a Rollercoaster

Let me get my thinking cap on and
Put two and two together,
'Cause I know that life is a rollercoaster.
You know what, Life, I know a trick or two, and
I can handle this.
You know what, Life, I know you inside out and
There is no need to pick someone's brain,
'Cause I am a walking encyclopedia.

I know my stuff, and
I am going to show you, Life, that knowledge is power.
I know that life is a journey, not a destination, and
I have all what it takes to endure all the difficult that
You, Life, keep on throwing at me.
I know that life is a box of chocolates, and
Life is not a bed of roses;
However, life is what you make it.

You know what, Life, don't judge someone by their
appearance, because you will be caught by surprise
To find it out the hard way that I am tough as old boots,
I am also having a heart of steel, and nerves of steel.
Forget that I am going to throw in the towel;
Instead, I am going to tough it out and
Push forward against all odds,

'Cause I am determined to succeed at all costs.

Come what may, I will soldier on and
Stand my ground.
Come hell or high water, I am going to stick to my guns,
'Cause I am determined to succeed.
I am going to zero in on my goals, and
I am not going to let myself get side-tracked,
'Cause I am unwavering committed to see this trough
To the end.

I am committed to go to great lengths for me to succeed,
And I promise that I will move heaven and earth for me to
Achieve my dreams.
I am going to pace myself, 'cause I know life is a marathon, not a sprint.
I am going to write my own history, 'cause life is a book.
I will remain resolute and display what I am made of,
'Cause life is a mirror, and
I will keep on fighting you, Life, until I do the trick.

75
Catch Me If You Can

I am sprinting like a cheater.
I am faster like lightning,
Catch me if you can.
I attack prey fast like falcon peregrine.
I am faster than the speed of sound,
Like supersonic aircraft.
I am the mirage,
Catch me if you can.
I am a fish in water.
I am invisible and strong like wind.
Chase me if you can and,
Be left for dust.

I am unstoppable like a warrior.,
I am full of boundless energy and,
Unwavering commitment to accomplishing my goals.
Stop me if you can.
I am tough as rock.
I am eager beave, and,
I am determined to overcome any obstacle,
That comes my way.
I am handful, Stop me if you can.
I am always ever-ready to toil away,
Come what may.